Technology Skills for Kids

– Technology Toolbox: Forms & Menus –

www.technologyskillsforkids.com

Hello and welcome!

This is **book #5** in a series of picture books created to help children make productive use of their computers and other devices while staying safe online.

"Happy Computer", Tech Wizard Mike & Tough Cookie

Due to space limitations (even in a **series of 12 books**), we have to paint these technology skills in very broad strokes.

Any words or phrases in **bold orange** are topics that will be explored further in this book's **supplemental materials**.

You will use the **technology basics** (see book #3) to interact with forms and menus.

Let's Go FORMal!

Yes, forms are boring. But there is not much you can do without them.

Paper forms may one day go the way of the dodo but methodical procedure and accuracy will always be essential.

Forms are very powerful!

An email message box is a form:

Please note the **functionalities** in the above form. For example, the "curved arrows" are redo and undo buttons.

Filling out a form on a device is conceptually the same as filling out a paper form (and really about as complicated).

When you set up a new device, you will need to fill out some forms.

And you should record the information you provide into those forms (e.g. your admin username and password) into your technology notebook.

Four common form slip-ups

1. Forgetting haste makes waste

Carefully read each part of the form before you click, tap or press any keys on your keyboard.

2. Not noting the passwords and usernames they created and/or the answers to the security questions that they selected

Yikes! This is where forms can come back to bite you!

3. Forgetting about context

You would not, for example, want to type one of your passwords into a first name box:

First name

Wizard123.

4. Pressing the Enter / Return key on the keyboard before the form is **completed** (and proofread for accuracy):

Fun fact: Pressing the **enter / return key** on your keyboard has the same result as clicking or tapping the form's "Submit" button:

And attempting to submit an **incomplete** form will generate some kind of error message and you may have to start all over again.

Contact form

Name

Email ID

Subject

Message

The Name field must contain only alphabets and space
The Email ID field must contain a valid email address
The Subject field is required
The Message field is required

Five tips for filling out forms

1. Proofread the completed form for accuracy **before** you submit it.

2. Remember that the blinking line is a **text insertion point**. It needs to be in any text box that you wish to type into.

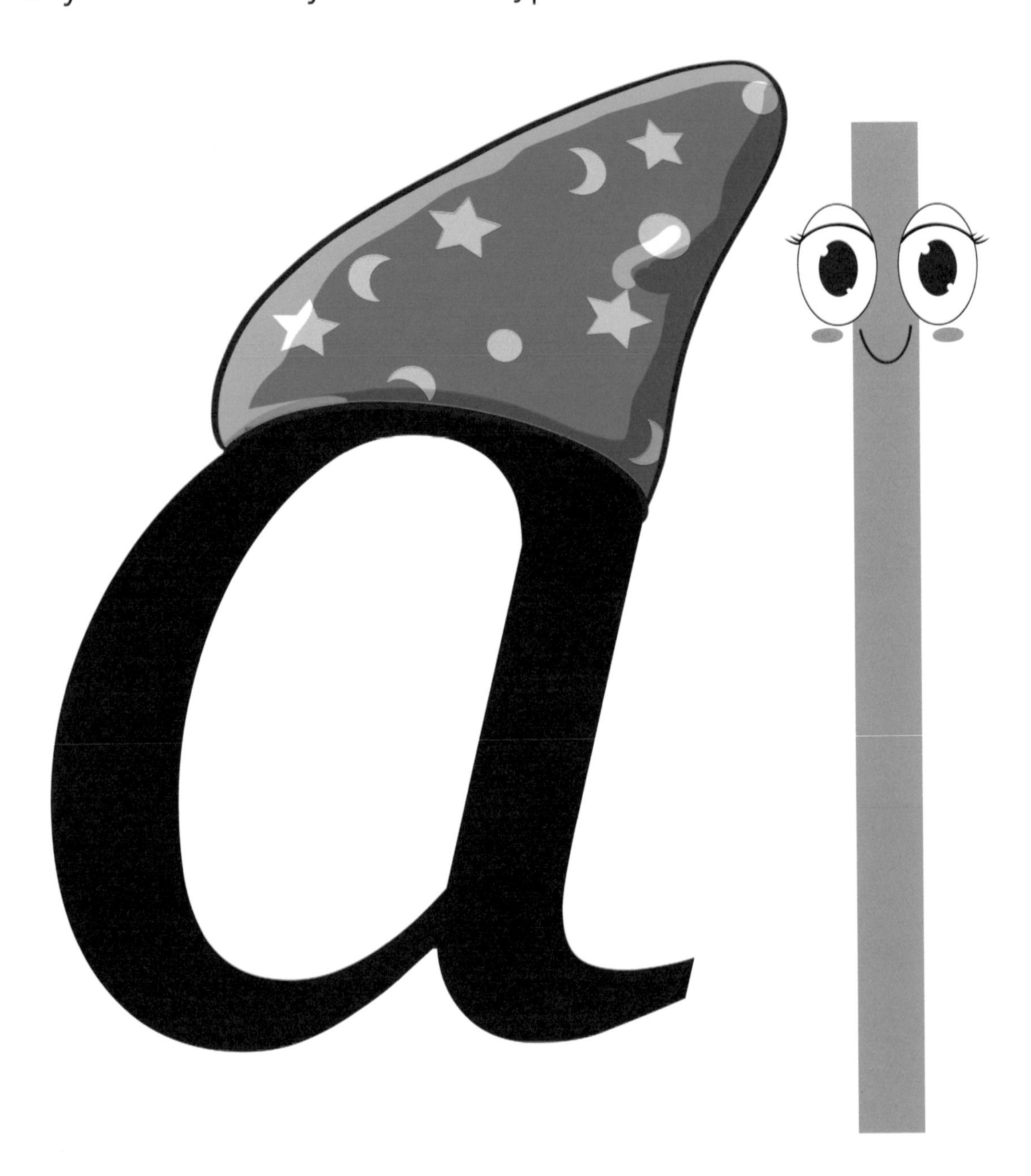

Please note the "blinking line" (highlighted below) in this web search box:

You can move the blinking line around a text box by pressing the **arrow keys** on your keyboard and by pressing the **backspace** key.

3. Ask yourself "**What is this form for?**" Is it for a cloud account? Is it for device login? Is it to administer the device? It is very important to understand exactly what a form is for. If you are uncertain about anything on a form, get some good help.

You do not want to be here! You do not want to find yourself staring at a login screen without a clue.

4. Carefully record any usernames and passwords you create for yourself (plus any additional information) into your designated **technology notebook**.

You may be at least a few years away from having a bank account but here we have a web address, a username, a password and an explanatory doodle – this system works!

5. Make sure you can see the entire form.

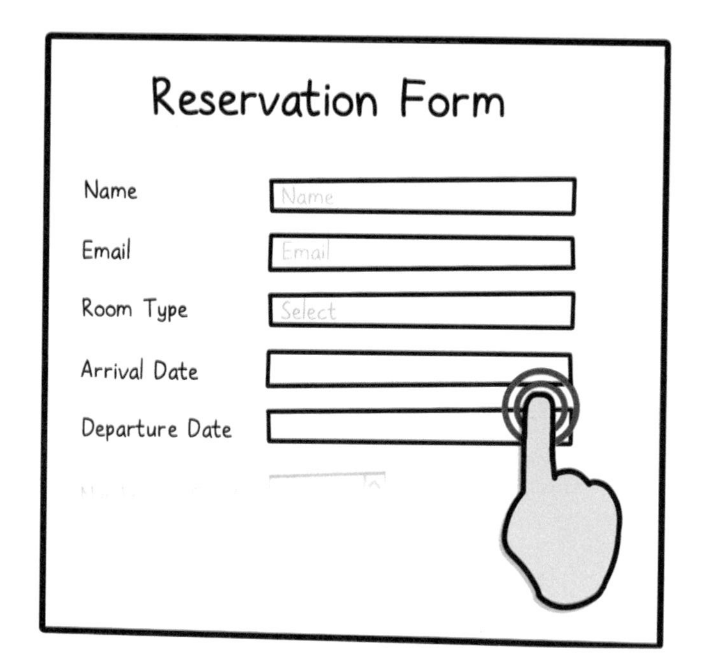

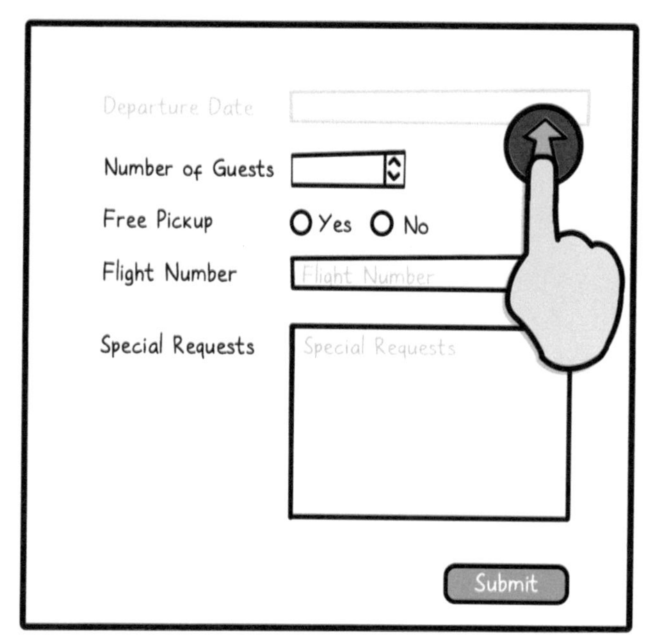

Think about what you want to do (e.g. scroll up a form) and then look around for a way to do it.

Menus

MENU
print
save
copy
paste
bookmark
help
share

Many apps will have menus…

Question: How do you find the various menus on your device?

Answer: Noodle around for them!

For example, clicking the Caret icon (^) on this particular computer screen revealed some "hidden" functionalities...

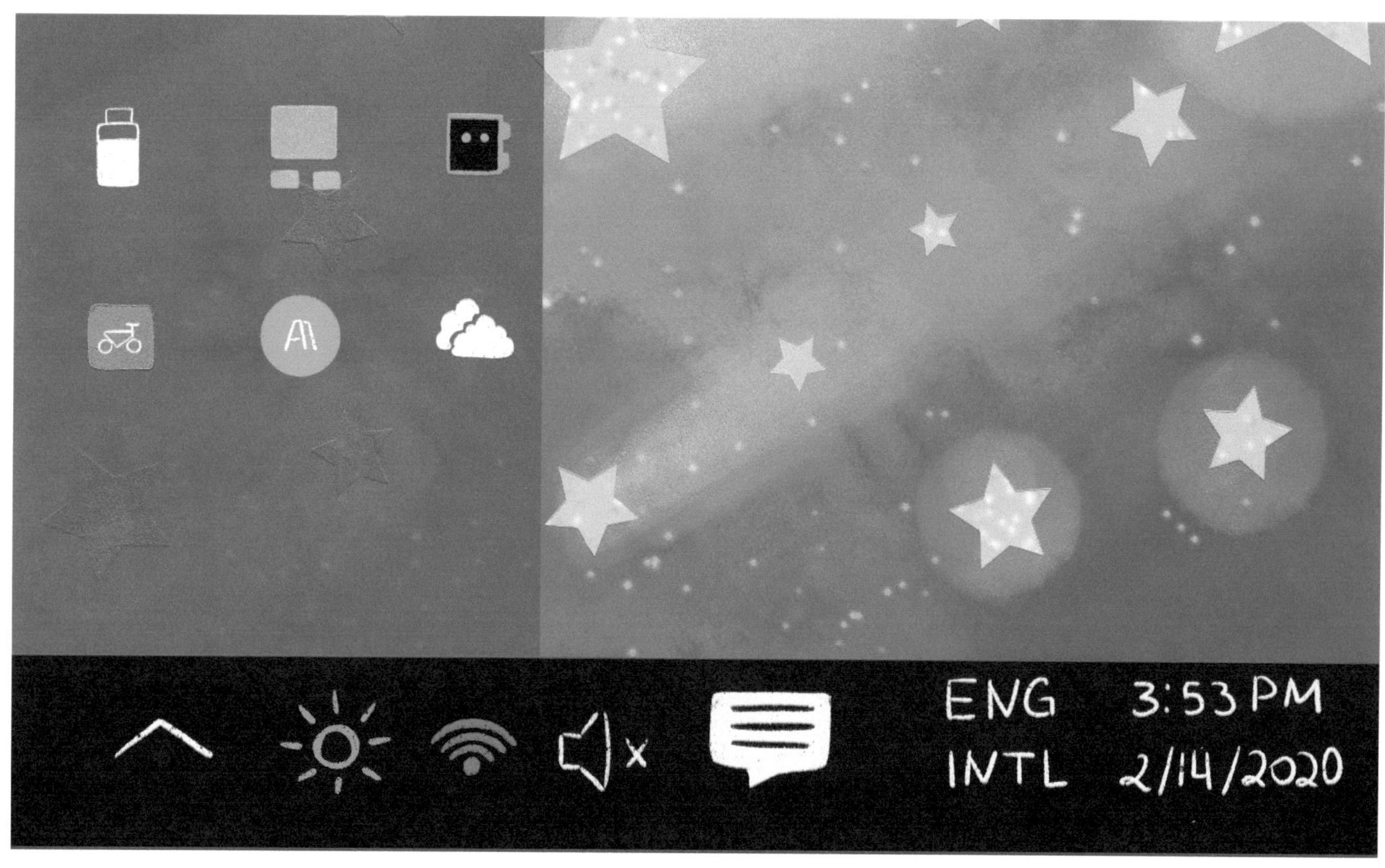

Meet "Mr. Context"!

Please note this mouse has two hands:

(And your mouse may have "two hands" as well – in the form of a left mouse button and a right mouse button.)

The **right button** on a mouse can be used to summon a **context menu**.

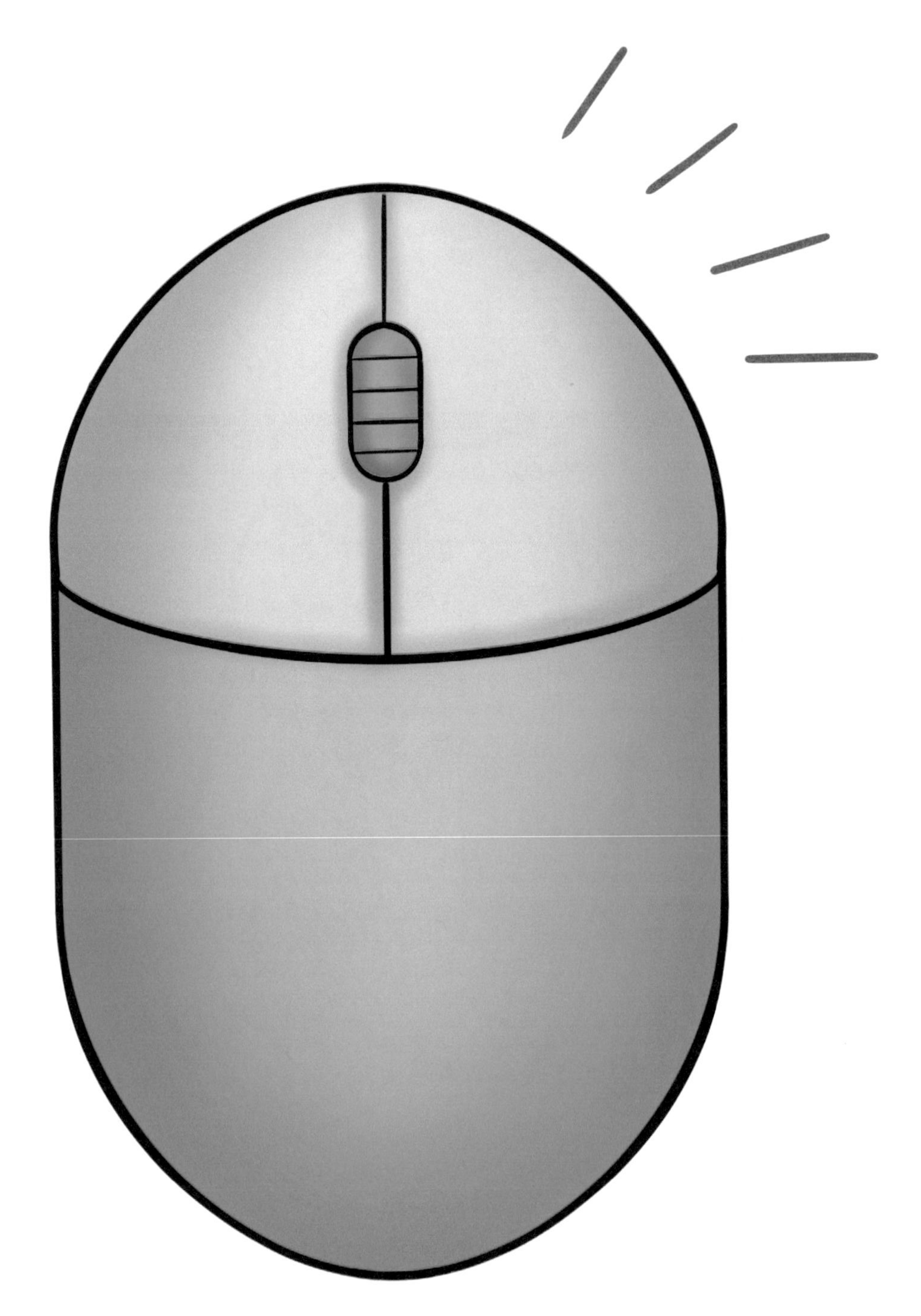

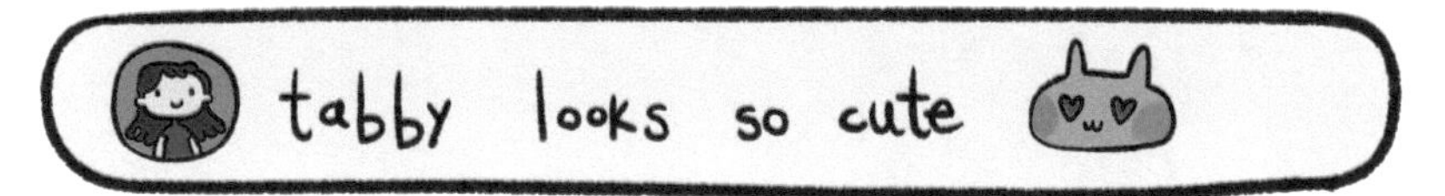

The selections on a context menu will **vary** depending on...

That's right! You guessed it!

Context!

The context menu can be called the secret agent technology tool because he is hidden until called.

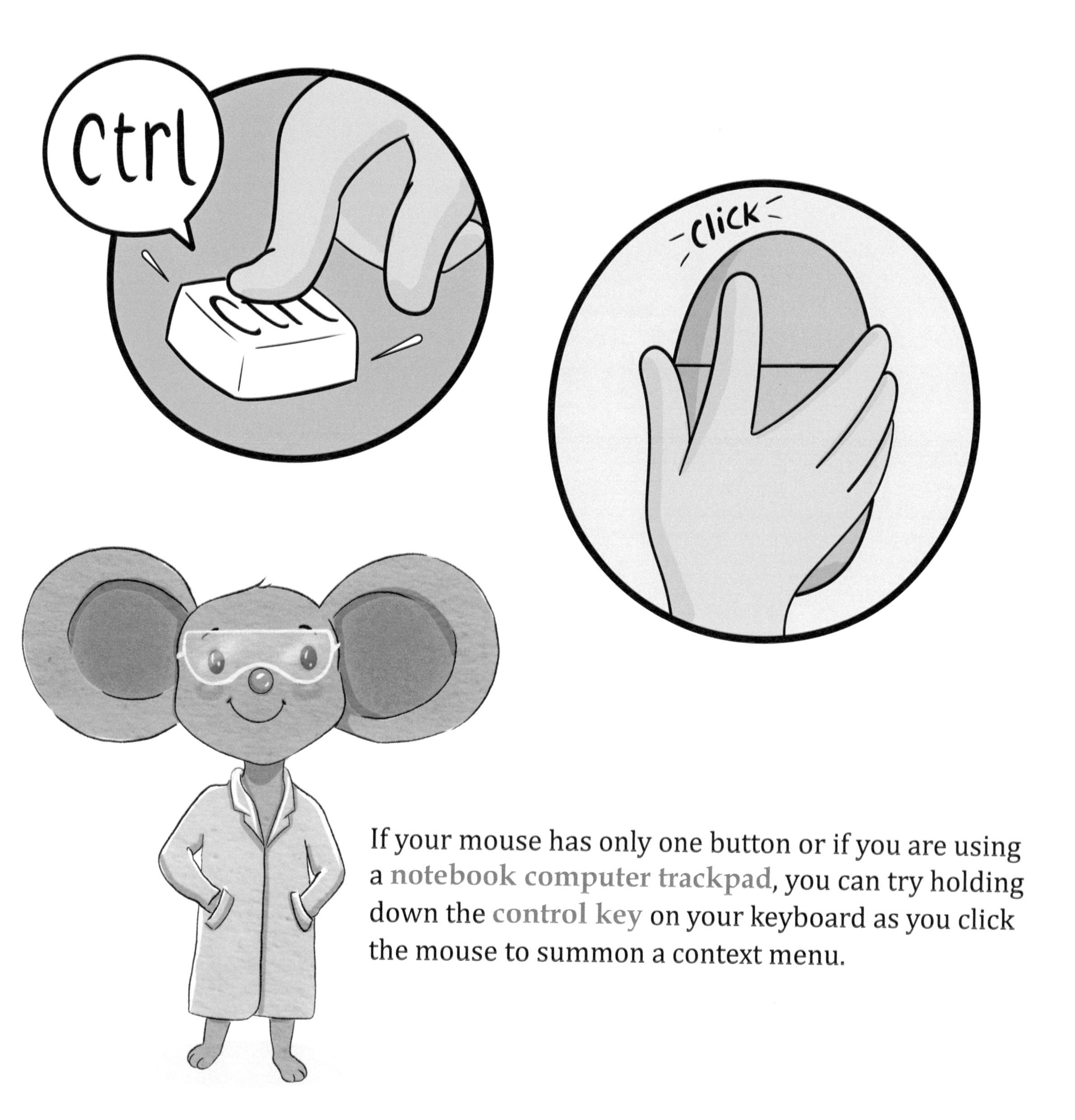

If your mouse has only one button or if you are using a **notebook computer trackpad**, you can try holding down the **control key** on your keyboard as you click the mouse to summon a context menu.

The "nuts & bolts" of technology use (e.g. how to summon a context menu) are not as important as a **conceptual understanding** of what you would like to accomplish.

"Sam the great tire changer"

Tap & hold

You can tap and hold over something (e.g. an **icon**) on a touch screen device to cause a context menu to appear:

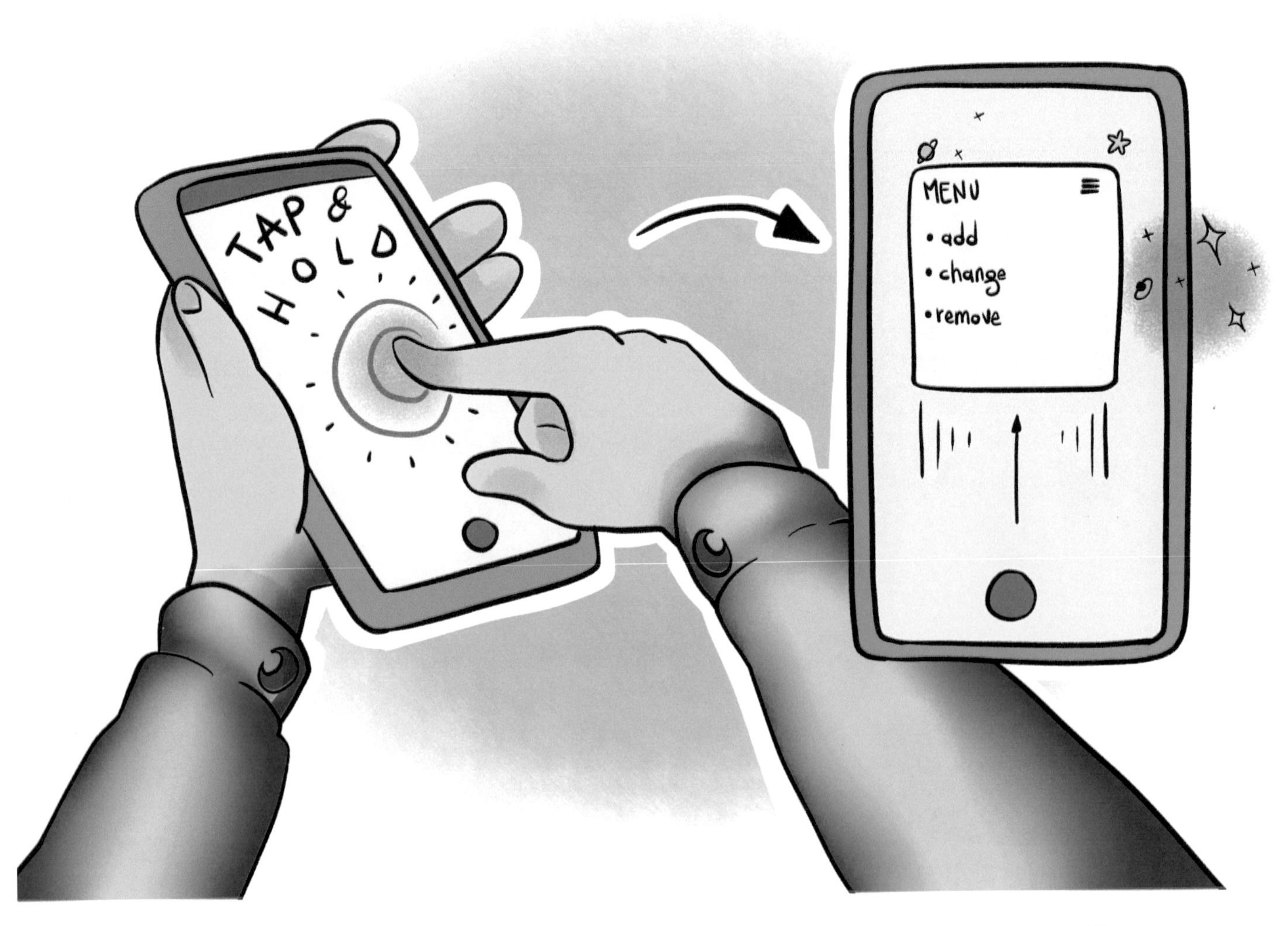

Tapping & holding on a touch screen device has the same effect as a **secondary mouse click** on a computer.

Context matters! The selections on a context menu will depend on which app you are using (if any) and what the tip of your finger is currently over.

Context menu on a smartphone

Methods for summoning context menus will vary between devices.

If you **know what you are using** (and you should), you can **search the web** for whatever you need to find out:

There is nothing magical about methodical procedure and carefully following visual cues.

(And to be honest, Tabby was not this impressed when Tech Wizard Mike demonstrated how to summon a context menu on a touch screen device.)

We may need to see the **complete picture** in order to get a very basic understanding of how all the parts fit together.

NO TIME TO EXPLAIN
GET IN THE CAR

Visit www.technologyskillsforkids.com for more tech skills for kids including blog posts, videos and book #6 in which we will begin our discussion of the "Technology Foundation."

Made in the USA
Columbia, SC
14 May 2024

35567260R00027